FRUITCAKE

FRUITCAKE

BY URSULA EVANS

with photography by
Richard Hammerton

To my mother

Copyright © 2015 Ursula Evans

First published in the UK in 2015

by Middle Farm Press

British Library Cataloguing-in-Publication Data

A catalogue record for this book is available from the British Library

ISBN 978-0-9928896-2-3

Designer: Kath Grimshaw

Photographer: Richard Hammerton

Editor: Kate Taylor

Printed in Italy

Published by Middle Farm Press

Middle Farm, Shropshire

www.middlefarmpress.com

CONTENTS

Acknowledgements

I am indebted to my mother – she taught me to reach for the stars and encouraged my passion and enthusiasm, not just for baking, but for life. Huge thanks must also go to my wonderful family who have always believed in me and support me in everything I do, and without whom all of this would not be possible; especially my husband Richard, backroom-boy extraordinaire, my son Matthew and his fiancée Luisa, my daughters Rhiannon and Catrin who are always willing to help me, my dad who has taken up the baton for baking in mum's absence, and my in-laws Alan and Shirley. I love you all.

Thanks to all my friends near and far, who constantly inspire me and encourage me and often test and critique my recipes.

Thank you to the fabulous and knowledgeable team at Middle Farm Press for creating this beautiful book; to Kate for her patience, editorial and management, Richard for his excellent photography, Kath for her unique design and Sam for her enthusiasm and encouragement. It has been very exciting working with all of you.

Thank you to all the lovely My Cottage Kitchen customers and fans without whom I wouldn't have a business; thank you for buying my fruitcakes and now for buying my book and baking fruitcakes yourselves!

Living the Dream

I smile when my daughters say "Mum you're living the dream", because they are right.

I faced a difficult decision when I was eighteen – should I choose a career in food technology or nursing. I chose the latter and subsequently had a very happy 30 years working in many different areas of nursing. It was through nursing that I met my husband and went on to have three children. Despite the relentless shift work and long awkward hours, my keen interest in cooking remained. My mother was the one who introduced me to cooking – I have very fond memories of baking in our kitchen together at a young age. I remember, at the age of seven, bravely baking rock cakes for my first Brownie badge!

I have gone on to nurture these interests in my children and, now grown-up, they are all very competent cooks. At university they would often delight their friends with dinner, and I would be the trouble-shooter at the end of the phone. Cooking is a sociable affair and I love it when they cook for me.

My husband and I live in the beautiful Shropshire countryside. We renovated an 1880s miner's cottage and have a productive cottage garden. This was undoubtedly the catalyst for my decision to work from home. My home business had to involve cooking and/or gardening, and My Cottage Kitchen was launched in 2010. Four years on I am baking at least 1,000 fruitcakes a year, I have won several awards and, most importantly, I am having a lot of fun.

So why fruitcakes? Well I have been baking fruitcakes for many years and I would rarely bake just one – it was normally an oven full and I would give them as gifts to family and friends. It was one of my husband's work colleagues who gave me the idea of selling them.

Running a Successful Home Business

My first tip for running a successful home business is to enjoy what you are doing, or at least most of it. The second is to pay great attention to detail. Running a food business from home involves registering with the local authority and following food safety regulations strictly. I initially found some helpful local courses for small business start-ups, but the best advice came just when I was beginning to feel daunted by business planning strategies; I was told to just 'get on with it', so I booked my first farmers market, made my first batch of fruitcakes and sold them to a very appreciative crowd at Harper Adams Farmers Market.

Fruitcakes are not just for Christmas

People laugh when I say "Fruitcakes aren't just for Christmas", but I feel that the traditional British fruitcake has had a very hard time. It did lose popularity for a while, but thanks to a revival of home baking there seems to be a real interest in traditional bakes. In this book I want to share my award-winning recipes, and some of our family favourites too, but also introduce new contemporary fruitcake recipes and give new ideas for decorating and serving. I want to demonstrate how easy it is to bake a fruitcake – you don't need to be a professional to bake a good fruitcake, but you do have to enjoy baking! I hope to inspire a new generation of fruitcake lovers who can find a fruitcake for every occasion, not just for Christmas!

What makes fruitcake special?

The quality of a fruitcake is determined by the ingredients it contains, and the time allocated to the preparation, baking and maturing process. I also believe that the passion and creativeness of the baker determines the quality of a fruitcake.

The actual definition of fruitcake is 'a cake containing dried fruits and nuts', and in botanical terms fruit is the sweet and fleshy edible product of a plant or tree containing seeds. Interestingly, when we think of fruitcakes we think of those made with dried fruits, but when we think of fruit we instantly think of the fruits in our fruit bowl. With this mind, I made the decision that for this book, any cake containing fruit, whether dried or fresh, is a fruitcake!

Rich fruitcakes really are very special cakes, they are packed full of dried fruits usually soaked in alcohol, fruit juice or tea. They also contain spices, butter, sugar, eggs and flour making them wholesome cakes that keep well. Rich fruitcakes are synonymous with special occasions, steeped in tradition, but are equally fitting for everyday cakes.

Always allow plenty of time to bake a rich fruitcake, but most of all, enjoy baking them. Use your imagination, and practice makes perfect. Don't be put off by disasters, we all have them but can learn from them. Experiment with different types of fruitcake, a savvy cook makes the most of fresh fruits at the height of their season, so why not bake fresh fruitcakes and freeze them. An adventurous cook looks for new and exciting recipes, so why not create your own new fruitcake with your favourite ingredients, or use edible flowers, fruit and vegetables from your garden.

The Ingredients

Butter

Butter is a fat made from cow's milk by separating the cream and churning it; it is a good source of fat-soluble vitamin A and D. It is flavoursome and easily creams with sugar at room temperature, introducing bubbles which are locked in during baking. Other types of fat can be used in baking fruitcakes, including oils which make very moist cakes; even margarines and lactose-free spreads have been used successfully to make fruitcakes.

*Salt is added to some butters but I have always used unsalted butter in my baking.

Sugar

Sugars are carbohydrates and come in many forms. Refined sugar is made from raw sugar after the molasses have been removed. Brown sugars are either unrefined or partially refined and are often used in baking fruitcakes to produce a pleasing taste and texture, and a dark colour. Natural sugars from fruits like dates and honey can be substituted for sugars, producing an equally-sweet taste in baking. Golden syrup and treacle are sugars made during the sugar refining process, treacle contains the most molasses and has a stronger taste and darker colour.

*I give weights in grams for treacle and syrup rather than tablespoons as I usually dispense them from squeezy bottles straight into the mix on my weighing scales; it saves a lot of mess and waste.

Dried Fruit

Retaining most of their natural sugar and minerals, dried fruits are a valuable source of calcium, iron and fibre, which aids digestion. Dried fruits have had most of their water removed either naturally by sun drying or mechanically. They are flavoursome and the biggest and most important ingredient in a rich fruitcake. They are easy to store in air-tight containers, which prevent them from drying out. The main ingredients of a rich fruitcake are the vine fruits – sultanas, raisins and currants, all three of which are dried varieties of grapes. Grapes have been grown for thousands of years and are predominantly grown for wine, but certain types of grapes are dried to produce sultanas, raisins and currants. They are an excellent source of antioxidants.

Currants: Dark red seedless grapes, sun-dried until tiny and shrivelled. Originally cultivated in southern Greece, the name comes from the ancient city of Corinth. I prefer to use Vostizza currants as they are the highest quality and very flavoursome.

Sultanas: Large white seedless grapes, some sultanas are mechanically dried in sulphur dioxide which produces the golden colour while others are sun-dried naturally. I prefer to use unsulphured sun-dried sultanas.

Raisins: White grapes, Thompson seedless are the most popular raisin, naturally sun-dried, producing the darker colour.

Citrus Rind (Zest) and Juice

Ripe, fresh fruits contain sugar and vitamin C, but unfortunately vitamin C is lost during the baking process. Fruit juice and zest are traditionally used in baking to add flavour.

Nuts

The nutritional value of nuts will vary depending on the type but, generally, nuts are highly nutritious containing protein, fat, minerals, dietary fibre and some vitamins (mainly vitamin B/thiamine). Oil in ground almonds helps keep cakes moist.

Once nuts are taken out of the shell they have a relatively short self life so I buy them in small quantities.

Eggs

Eggs increase the food value of dishes they are added to. They contain protein and fat, and provide substantial amounts of vitamin A and D and small amounts of other vitamins and minerals. The most important properties of eggs in baking are their ability to hold air, adding lightness to cakes, and their coagulation and thickening action which holds cakes together.

Eggs should always be at room temperature before use. I love using my own eggs from my rare-breed chickens – their yolks are always a lovely dark yellow colour because they graze on grass most of the day. If I buy eggs they are always free-range.

Flour

Depending on the type of flour, the nutritional value will vary, but generally white flour is mainly carbohydrate with some protein, vitamins and minerals. The more processed the flour, the less nutritional value remains as the proteins contained in the grain are removed. Wholegrain flours contain more dietary fibre, too. Wheat flour is very important in baking cakes because it forms an elastic cake batter that is subsequently raised by air or carbon dioxide as the cake bakes. Sifting the flour incorporates more air. Wheat and gluten-free flour blends available in many shops these days can be substituted in most of my recipes and I have used them to bake my fruitcakes with ease. The texture is slightly different but otherwise the fruitcakes are similar.

*I like to use plain and self-raising flours which are lower in gluten and starchier; they absorb fat better making them good for cakes.

Spice

Spices have distinctive strong flavours. They are traditionally added to fruitcakes and have been used in cooking for hundreds of years. They were introduced to Britain by the Romans, and imported mainly from the Far East. Freshly-ground spices have more flavour. It is best to buy them in small quantities as they do lose flavour quickly.

*Shop-purchased blends often include ingredients such as ground coriander, ground caraway, mace and cardamom.

Alcohol

Although alcohol can be utilised as a source of energy, it has very little nutritional benefit. Traditionally, however, spirits have been used to add flavour and extend the shelf life of fruitcakes, by preventing mould growth.
I like to use a VSOP blend of brandy, matured in oak barrels, for flavouring my awarding-winning fruitcakes.

Raising Agents

Mechanically – introducing air by sifting or trapping air in creaming butter and sugar or by whisking eggs to form foam.
Chemically – producing carbon dioxide bubbles during baking, e.g. baking powder and bicarbonate of soda, although the later has a bitter taste and is only used in cakes with strong flavours. Self-raising flour already has the raising agent added.
Baking powder can be made by combining 2 tsp cream of tartar with 1 tsp bicarbonate of soda. Commercial baking powder does have a filler (usually corn flour) so you may need a quarter of a tsp less for most recipes if you make your own.

AGA Baking

My AGA cooker is the 4 oven heat storage type and it is on all the time, however, if you have a Total Control AGA the oven will need preheating just like conventional ovens.

Pudding Spice:

This is a traditional English blend of spices, also known as pudding spice, often used in fruitcakes, Christmas puddings, mincemeat and hot cross buns. Although it can be easily purchased ready-mixed, some cooks prefer to make their own, experimenting with the flavours, emphasizing certain spices depending on the dish they are preparing.

This is my favourite aromatic blend, it is a traditional blend but don't make too much, as spices tend to lose flavour if kept for too long.

1 tbsp Ground Cinnamon
1 tbsp Ground Ginger
1 tbsp Ground Nutmeg
½ tbsp Ground Cloves
½ tbsp Allspice

Mix all the spices above together and store in an airtight jar.

Useful Utensils

Handwash
Use unscented antibacterial handwash to avoid transferring a scent to the food when handling fruit or kneading and moulding sugar paste or marzipan.

Electric Mixer
Electric mixers save time and energy, but are not essential. They are available in attractive designs as complete stand-alone mixers, hand mixers or food processors. It is best to choose one depending on how you intend to use it because they can do a lot more than just mix cake mixture.

Mixing Bowls
I recommend more than one large bowl and several small bowls as many recipes require multiple bowls. I like ceramic bowls that are oven, microwave, freezer and dishwasher proof.

Spoons
I can't imagine a kitchen without spoons – metal, wooden or silicone, they are absolutely essential for beating and mixing. Metal spoons should always be used for folding flour and whisked eggs into a mix.

Spatula
A bendy spatula is a great utensil because it quickly and easily removes most of the cake mixture from the bowl with little waste.

Weighing Scales
Accuracy is important in baking so good weighing scales are essential. These can be electronic/battery digital or traditional balance scales. It is useful to have scales that will measure down to 1 gram or at least 5 grams.

Sieves
Use a large sieve for sifting flour – essential for getting air into the cake mixture. Use a small tea strainer for dusting cakes.

Skewers
A metal skewer is used to determine whether a cake is completely baked in the middle.

Baking Tins
These come in all shapes and sizes and are made from different materials too. I prefer heavy-duty ones because I use them a lot. There are specialist shops that will hire out tins if you need a large tin or an unusually-shaped one for a one-off celebration cake. It is always worth following the manufacturer's instructions for care.

Scissors
I use a good pair of kitchen scissors for cutting dried fruit like apricots and figs; it is easier and quicker than using a knife for small amounts.

Zester
As fruitcakes often require citrus zest, a good-quality grater or zester is essential.

Juicer
After using the zester the citrus fruit will often require juicing, so a simple juicer is very handy.

Baking Parchment/ Greaseproof Paper
Parchment is non-stick paper ideal for lining cake tins. It is moistureproof and greaseproof making it good for wrapping fruitcake while maturing. If you use greaseproof paper you may need to add some additional grease to adhere the paper to the tin when lining.

Cooling Racks
For the even cooling of all-sized cakes and the prevention of condensation formation, it is important to use a cooling rack.

Spray Oils
These are great for spraying a light layer on tins before lining them; the alternative is using a small piece of paper with a small piece of butter to run around the tin.

Pestle and Mortar
Very useful for crushing and grinding spices. Can be wooden, ceramic or stone but need to be heavy and strong.

Knives

It is useful to have a selection of knives for different tasks – palate knives are great for spreading on icings; serrated knives should be used for cutting fruitcakes; pizza wheels can be useful for cutting sugar and almond paste; small sharp knives are required frequently for various tasks such as cutting and chopping. All knives should be carefully stored and maintained.

I like to use knives, forks and spoons to create edgings to marzipan and sugar paste, and I still tend to use these in preference to some of my professional decorating tools.

Timer

When the children are cooking they use their mobile phones. I prefer using my wind-up timer and do so several times a day; I can wash it regularly and it sticks on the fridge. It is so easy to forget I have things in the oven because I bake most days and fruitcakes also take a long time to bake so you can easily get involved in other projects and forget them.

Clothing

Wear a white T-shirt when decorating cakes because strange as it may seem, small fibres from dark clothes can get rolled into the sugar paste. Equally, it is a good idea to wear aprons and short-sleeved tops when baking, which I do as routine for my business. I wear a hat too!

Dredger

This is an easy way to spread a light dusting of icing sugar over the work surface before rolling out the sugar paste.

Plastic Smoothers

Inexpensive and useful for levelling and smoothing sugar paste, if you want a good finish you will need these.

Cutters

There is a huge assortment of cutters available to buy at a fairly low cost these days, and I have quite a collection of them now, but tend to use only my favourite ones. You don't really need a lot of them unless you are going to be decorating a lot of cakes.

Brushes

A good selection of pastry brushes, for brushing the cakes with glaze and alcohol, and different sizes of painting brushes are useful when decorating, not just for painting with edible paint.

Rolling Pins

These are essential for rolling out marzipan and sugar paste and it is useful to have a couple of sizes, too. All kitchens need a rolling pin but if it goes missing I have seen a jam jar being used successfully.

Whisk

Whether electric or hand-propelled, a whisk is essential for whisking eggs and other mixes and no kitchen should be without one.

Wooden Boards

If your work surface isn't suitable for rolling out then a wooden board is useful.

Plastic Bags

Sugar paste goes hard very quickly so when not in use it should always be wrapped in a plastic bag.

Blowtorch

I use a blowtorch for finishes to marzipan decorations, it is also great for puddings like Crème brûlée but it isn't an essential tool. However, once you have one you will wonder how you ever managed without it.

Umbrella Cake Covers

These inexpensive covers are great for covering cakes while the marzipan or icing is drying.

AWARD-WINNING RECIPES

These are my award-winning recipes.
Tried and tested thousands of times.
Follow my instructions carefully and
you will bake the best fruitcake ever!

This is the original fruitcake, the one that inspired everything from starting the business to writing this book.

WINNER
BEST CAKE
CARFEST 2012
GREAT TASTE AWARD 2011

TRADITIONAL RICH FRUITCAKE

INGREDIENTS	15cm round Large loaf tin	20cm round 15cm square 2 large loaf tins 15 mini cake cases	25cm round 20cm square 4 large loaf tins 30 mini cake cases
Sultanas	175g	350g	700g
Raisins	150g	300g	600g
Currants	100g	200g	400g
Large orange (zest and juice)	1	2	4
Brandy	50mls	100mls	200mls
Natural-coloured glacé cherries	50g	100g	200g
Treacle	25g	50g	100g
Golden syrup	25g	50g	100g
Demerara sugar	90g	180g	360g
Unsalted butter	115g	230g	460g
Free-range eggs	2	4	8
Plain flour	50g	100g	200g
Self-raising flour	90g	180g	360g
Mixed spice	1/2 tbsp	1 tbsp	2 tbsp
Ground almonds	25g	50g	100g
Flaked almonds	25g	50g	100g
Bake slowly at a low temperature: Conventional oven 140c Fan oven 120c Gas Mark 1	2 – 2½ hours	2 ½ – 3 hours	3 – 3 ½ hours
AGA – start in baking oven for 30 mins then move to simmering oven	6 – 8 hours	8 – 10 hours	10 – 12 hours
Brandy to pour over each week	15mls	30mls	60mls

PREPARATION

1. First measure out the vine fruits – sultanas, raisins and currants – into a large bowl and remove any stalks. These days most vine fruits are already washed, however, if not they will need to be washed and drained through a sieve and dried well, to prevent mould growth during maturing.

2. Grate the orange zest carefully avoiding the bitter pith, then cut the oranges in half and extract the juice and add to the vine fruits; add the brandy and mix well.

3. Cover and leave the fruits to soak overnight until they are plump, and most of the brandy and orange juice has been absorbed.

LINING THE TIN

Grease and line a deep baking tin with greaseproof paper or baking parchment.

MIXING

1. The following day add the glacé cherries, treacle and golden syrup to the soaked fruits and mix well. They will smell delicious.

2. Make sure the eggs and butter are at room temperature for at least 30 minutes before using them. Preheat conventional ovens and turn on iTotal AGA cookers.

3. Measure out all the dry ingredients and set aside.

4. Using an electric mixer cream together the demerara sugar and unsalted butter until light and fluffy, this can be done by hand but it will take at least 10 minutes.

5. Next add the eggs one at a time with a spoonful of flour to prevent curdling. Then gently mix in all the dry ingredients, and finally the soaked vine fruit mixture. Spoon the mixture into the prepared baking tin and level the top.

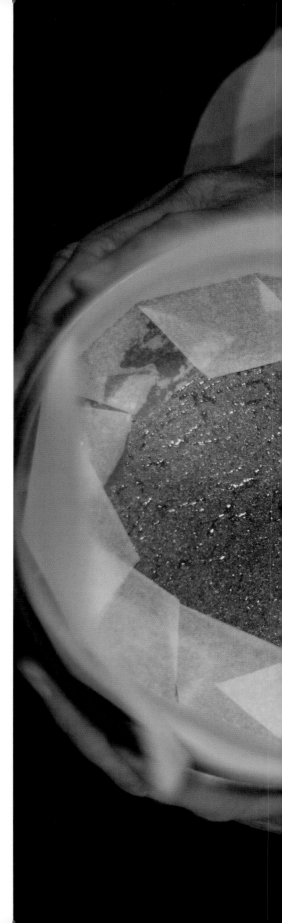

BAKING

1. The best way to bake a rich fruitcake is slowly at a low temperature; in conventional ovens you may need to cover the cake during the last hour to prevent the top from burning.

2. In AGA cookers the baking starts off in the baking oven and is moved to the simmering oven but the baking time depends on the running temperature of individual AGA cookers.

3. The baked fruitcake should look brown, and should be shrinking away from the sides of the tin; it should feel firm on top and smell cooked, there should be no bubbling sounds and a skewer inserted into the middle should come out clean.

4. Leave the cake in the tin to cool. Pour over a little brandy while the cake is hot if you wish.

MATURING

1. Leave the greaseproof lining paper on the cake and wrap in a second layer, then wrap in two layers of food wrap.

2. Store the cake at room temperature to mature for at least four weeks, unwrapping and wrapping again on a weekly basis to add more brandy. Invert or turn upside down from time to time. This keeps the top flat and evens out the moisture of the cake.

3. As the cake matures you will notice it becoming dark and sticky. This fruitcake will keep for up to one year if stored correctly and alcohol has been added regularly.

GREAT
TASTE
AWARD
2012

I created this for those who prefer less refined
sugar, and it tastes sweet enough with just the
natural sugars from the fruits and dates.

NATURALLY SWEETENED FRUITCAKE

INGREDIENTS	15cm round Large loaf tin	20cm round 15cm square 2 large loaf tins 15 mini cake cases	25cm round 20cm square 4 large loaf tins 30 mini cake cases
Dates: chopped and made into paste with water	90g 2 tbsp water	180g 4 tbsp water 350g	360g 8 tbsp water
Sultanas	175g	350g	700g
Raisins	150g	300g	600g
Currants	100g	200g	400g
Large orange (zest and juice)	1	2	4
Brandy	50mls	100mls	200mls
Unsalted butter	115g	230g	460g
Free-range eggs	2	4	8
Plain flour	50g	100g	200g
Self-raising flour	90g	180g	360g
Mixed spice	1/2 tbsp	1 tbsp	2 tbsp
Ground almonds	25g	50g	100g
Flaked almonds	25g	50g	100g
Bake slowly at a low temperature: Conventional oven 140c Fan oven 120c Gas Mark 1	2 – 2½ hours	2½ – 3 hours	3 – 3½ hours
AGA – start in baking oven for 30 mins then move to simmering oven	4 – 6 hours	6 – 8 hours	8 – 10 hours
Brandy to pour over each week	15mls	30mls	60mls

PREPARATION

1. Cut the dates in half and place in a saucepan, add the water and gently heat, stirring all the time until the dates become a paste, then leave to cool in a covered bowl overnight.

2. As with my traditional fruitcake, measure out the sultanas, raisins, and currants, remove any stalks and place in a bowl, grate the orange zest carefully avoiding the bitter pith, cut and extract the juice and add to vine fruit. Add the brandy and mix well, cover and leave to soak overnight until most of the brandy and orange juice has been soaked up.

LINING THE TIN

Grease and line a deep baking tin with greaseproof paper or baking parchment.

MIXING

1. Make sure the eggs and butter are at room temperature for at least 30 minutes before using them. Preheat conventional ovens and remember to turn on iTotal AGA cookers.

2. Measure out all the dry ingredients and set aside.

3. Using an electric mixer cream together the date paste and unsalted butter until light and fluffy, this doesn't take as long as creaming sugar and butter.

4. Next add the eggs one at a time with a spoonful of flour to prevent curdling. Then gently mix in all the dry ingredients and finally the soaked vine fruit mixture.

5. Spoon the mixture into the prepared baking tin and level the top.

BAKING

1. Bake this fruitcake slowly at a low temperature. It may need to be covered with greaseproof paper during the last hour to prevent the top from burning in conventional ovens.

2. In AGA cookers the baking starts off in the baking oven and moves to the simmering oven. Baking times may vary from one AGA cooker to another, so during the last hour it is best to check the fruitcake regularly.

3. The baked fruitcake should look brown, and should be shrinking away from the sides of the tin; it should feel firm on top and smell cooked, there should be no bubbling sounds and a skewer inserted into the middle should come out clean.

4. Leave the cake in the tin to cool. You may pour over a little brandy while the cake is hot if you wish.

MATURING

1. Leave the greaseproof paper on the cake and wrap in a second layer, then wrap in two layers of food wrap.

2. Store the cake at room temperature to mature for at least four weeks, unwrapping and wrapping again on a weekly basis to add more brandy.

3. As the cake matures you will notice it becoming darker and sticky with a delicious smell. This fruitcake will keep for six months if stored correctly.

DECORATING IDEAS

Rich fruitcakes are packed full of flavour and
can be enjoyed with simple or elaborate decorations.
A colourful arrangement of dried fruits and nuts
with apricot and brandy glaze has become my
signature fruitcake decoration. In a similar way,
whole glacé fruits can also be used on top of a layer
of almond paste. Be as creative as you wish;
you don't need to be an expert.

Often, celebration fruitcakes are covered in a marzipan base layer and then a layer of either sugar paste or royal icing, and then decorated to denote the occasion. The decorations can be made from hand moulding sugar paste to create flowers or figures, or by crystallising flowers, or hand painting using edible paint - this is much easier than piping icing. Write your ideas down or draw them first and practice them, but remember most decorations can be made in advance.

It would be a shame to decorate the No Added Sugar Fruitcake with a sugary icing, so I would recommend a simple edible flower or fruit arrangement which can be used effectively or just a thin covering of marzipan made with honey, or with a light drizzle of honey. It would also be perfect stacked between cheese truckles, and decorated with fruit, edible flowers and served with a jar of homemade chutney.

To the right is a guide to approximately how much of each to use depending on the size of the cake. The cake will need to be brushed with apricot glaze to help the marzipan stick to the cake and the almond paste allowed to dry for 24 hours before applying the sugar paste or royal icing. Sugar paste decorations can be applied to the iced cake with a brushing of water or vodka, and if the decorations are made in advance they will be dry so a paste can be made by mixing in a few drops of water or vodka with a little sugar paste, and this can be used as a glue to stick the decorations on.

Royal icing is a thick glossy covering for cakes and it sets very hard but can have glycerine added to give a softer set. It can be coloured with concentrated edible food colouring added in very small quantities and built up bit by bit to achieve the right colour. Always use a metal spoon to mix the icing to avoid mixing in air bubbles.

Sugar paste can be coloured by adding streaks of concentrated colour across the white sugar paste and then kneading it in until an even colour is achieved. I keep ready-made sugar paste in my cupboard in the primary colours - red, yellow and blue - as most colours I need can be quickly mixed by kneading these primary colours together. My daughters love decorating cakes and spend many happy hours creating their own designs. On a lightly dusted board roll out the sugar paste and using the cutter of choice press and twist gently to form the shape then push the shape out onto a dusted area.

Guide to covering celebration cakes	15cm round Large loaf tin	20cm round 15cm square 2 large loaf tins 15 mini cake cases	25cm round 20cm square 4 large loaf tins 30 mini cake cases
Almond Paste	600g	800g	1kg
Sugar Paste	800g	1kg	1.2kg
Royal Icing	2 egg whites	3 egg whites	4 egg whites

APRICOT JAM
(Using Fresh Apricots)

INGREDIENTS

3kg fresh apricots
450ml water
Juice of 1 lemon
3kg granulated sugar

A scum usually forms when air is trapped in the jam, so when the jam is taken off the heat stir it well and the bubbles should disappear. Jam should keep for more than a year, but it may loose its colour and flavour and start to dry out after a year. The keeping quality of jam is dependent on the proportion of sugar, the boiling and correct storage. It is important to use ripe or unripe fruit for jam making, never overripe fruit as it contains pectic acid which has no setting action. The fruit should also be picked in dry weather to reduce the growth of moulds and yeasts.

Boiled apricot jam is used to stick the almond paste to the cake, and also combined with brandy for glazing the fruits and nuts. If you would like to make your own jam it is very easy to make. Fresh apricots have plenty of pectin for setting, so an equal amount of fruit to sugar can be used.

1. Wash the apricots and halve them to remove the stone. Put the apricots, water and lemon juice in a pan and simmer until the apricots are softened.
2. Warm the sugar in a low oven while the apricots are simmering to help it dissolve quickly. Stir in the warmed sugar until dissolved and then boil rapidly to setting point.
3. To test the jam for setting point you can use a thermometer (the temperature should reach 104c), or put a teaspoon of jam on a cold saucer and push it across the saucer, if it wrinkles while tepid it should set.
4. Filling the jars is easier if the jars are placed on a tray close to the jam pan and the jam can then be quickly scooped up with a jug and poured into the sterilized jars.
5. Fill the jars to the top and place wax discs on top; these should be added immediately after filling the jars, with the waxed side in contact with jam. Clean the rim, and seal with a lid or cellophane.

*Makes approximately 6 x 200g jars.

BRANDY GLAZE

INGREDIENTS

2 tbsp apricot jam

1–2 tbsp brandy

1. To make a brandy glaze, put the apricot jam in a saucepan and heat gently until it melts then boil rapidly for about 60 seconds, this prevents mould growth.

2. Remove from the heat and stir in the brandy, pour it through a sieve to remove the apricot pieces, and store in a sterilized screw-top jar in the fridge until required.

3. Brush over dried fruit and nuts once arranged on the cake. It can also be used to coat the cake before applying marzipan.

*For an alcohol-free glaze use boiled water instead of brandy.

I don't like waste so I often don't sieve my own glaze because I don't mind the odd piece of apricot and often they sit at the bottom of the glaze anyway, but if you do sieve them out don't throw them away! They are delicious added to plain yogurt.

APRICOT JAM
(Using Dried Apricots)

Fresh apricots are not always available and this is a good recipe using dried apricots.

Dried apricots don't have as much pectin as fresh, so I recommend using a preserving sugar with added pectin. Unsulphured apricots are preferable as sulphured apricots are preserved with sulphur dioxide which has antimicrobial properties and prevents oxidization of dried fruits. Unsulphured apricots are naturally dark brown and very tasty, and sulphured apricots are an attractive bright orange, but some people are sensitive to the preservative, especially those with asthma.

1. Cut the apricots into small pieces – I find using scissors is the easiest way – and leave them to soak in the water for 24 hours.
2. Put the plump apricots and water into a pan and gently cook until soft.
3. Add the lemon juice, sugar and stir over a low heat until dissolved.
4. Boil rapidly to setting point.
5. Pour into hot sterilised jars and place wax discs on top; these should be added immediately after filling the jars, with the waxed side in contact with jam. Seal with lids.

*Makes approximately 6 x 200g jars.

INGREDIENTS

500g dried apricots
1.5 litres water
Juice of 1 lemon
1.5kg preserving sugar with added pectin

ALMOND PASTE
(Traditional)

Almond paste is easily available in the shops but many people don't realise how quick and easy it is to make, and the homemade version is always taster.

1. Mix the almonds and sugars together, make a well in the centre and pour in the beaten egg with almond essence and combine to make a soft paste.
2. Knead until smooth. It can be stored in a plastic bag to prevent drying out.

INGREDIENTS
200g ground almonds
100g golden caster sugar
100g icing sugar
1 egg
1 tsp almond essence
*makes approximately 500g

ALMOND PASTE
(Honey)

This recipe for an almond paste using honey instead of sugar makes a perfect topping for my No Added Sugar Fruitcake.

Put all the ingredients into a bowl and mix well then knead to a smooth paste.

INGREDIENTS
200g ground almonds
4 tbsp clear honey
1 tbsp lemon juice
*makes approximately 300g

ROYAL ICING

Perfect for classic snow scenes. As long as you have a good almond paste base layer, just spread it on, making peaks with the back of a spoon.

1. Whisk egg whites and lemon juice in a bowl until soft peaks form, work in 1/2 of the sifted sugar and whisk again. Lemon juice strengthens the egg white.
2. Work in more sifted sugar gradually until it looks glossy like whipped cream.
3. Cover with cling film and leave for 10 minutes to allow the bubbles to escape.
4. Add the glycerine and mix well with a metal spoon, this will make the icing softer and easier to cut. The icing is now ready to use

INGREDIENTS
2 egg whites
500g icing sugar *(sifted)*
1 tsp glycerine
½ tsp lemon juice

QUICK SUGAR PASTE

This is very easy to make and it can be rolled out and applied to the fruitcake over a base layer of almond paste.

1. Mix all ingredients together and knead until smooth and pliable.
2. Brush the almond paste with brandy, lightly dust a worktop with icing sugar and roll out the sugar paste to a circle, slightly bigger than the top of the cake.
3. Lift the sugar paste carefully over the cake and smooth out with your hands to help it stick.
4. Smooth the top and sides and use a knife to trim off any excess.

INGREDIENTS
500g icing sugar *(sifted)*
1 egg lightly beaten
30mls warmed liquid glucose
1 tsp glycerine
Sifted icing sugar for kneading

CRYSTALLISED FLOWERS

Primroses, violets, polyanthus, roses, pansies, carnation petals, mimosas, cowslips, sweet peas, fruit blossom and borage are all perfect for crystallising. Primroses are the easiest to handle. Crystallised flowers keep for several weeks and also retain their colour. Pick the flowers in the morning but when it is dry. Definitely don't use commercial flowers because they will have been sprayed with pesticides and are not intended for human consumption. Flowers from bulbs should not be eaten as they are poisonous.

1. Lightly beat the egg white with the vodka.
2. Handle the flowers carefully so they don't bruise and, using a small paintbrush, apply the beaten egg to both sides of each flower. Cover as much surface area as possible, then gently sprinkle over the sugar.
3. Dry on a wire rack for 24 hours before using to decorate your cake.

INGREDIENTS

1 egg white
½ tps vodka
Fresh edible flowers from the garden
500g fine caster sugar

APPLE CHUTNEY

Chutney is a hot sweet pickle originally from India, where it usually contains mangoes and chillies. It always includes fruit, spices, vinegar and sugar, and is cooked until it has the consistency of jam but it doesn't set. Chutney is an unusual condiment for fruitcake but works well when the fruitcake is served with cheese, as it is in Yorkshire.

1. Put vinegar, sugar, salt, mixed spice, ginger and pepper into a pan and bring to the boil.

2. Add the apples, onions, dates and figs and simmer without a lid for at least an hour, until the chutney is dark and a jam-like consistency. It is important to keep stirring frequently over a gentle heat otherwise the chutney easily burns.

3. Fill hot sterilised jars and seal with vinegar-proof lids.

INGREDIENTS

425mls dark malt vinegar

170g dark brown sugar

2 tsp salt

1 tsp mixed spice

2 tsp ground ginger

½ tsp cayenne pepper

500g apples peeled, cored and cut into small pieces

250g onion, chopped into small pieces

125g dates, cut into small pieces

125g dried figs, cut into small pieces

*Makes 4 x 400g jars

RICH FRUITCAKES

A good rich fruitcake will take time and patience
to make but will be well worth the effort.
Providing you store it correctly, you will
be rewarded with a fruitcake that will keep
for months, and as it matures the
flavours will develop.

The fruits and nuts I would normally use to decorate my original fruitcakes have gone into the mixture of this cake, making it a very rich and special fruitcake with the addition of dark and white chocolate, too.

VALENTINES TWO-CHOCOLATE FRUITCAKE

INGREDIENTS	Deep heart shaped tin, 21cm at widest part and 20cm long
Sultanas	200g
Raisins	200g
Currants	200g
Figs (chopped into small pieces)	75g
Prunes (chopped into small pieces)	75g
Dried apricots (chopped into small pieces)	75g
Mixed peel	50g
Oranges (zest and juice)	2
Brandy	100mls
Natural-coloured glacé cherries	75g
Treacle	50g
Golden syrup	50g
Demerara sugar	180g
Unsalted butter	230g
Free-range eggs	4
Plain flour	100g
Self-raising flour	180g
Mixed spice	1 tbsp
Ground almonds	50g
Flaked almonds	50g
Chopped pecans	50g
Whole pistachios	50g
White chocolate (roughly chopped)	75g
Dark chocolate 85% cocoa solids (roughly chopped)	75g
Brandy to pour over each week	30mls

Bake slowly at
a low temperature:
Conventional oven 140c
Fan oven 120c
Gas Mark 1
2½ – 3 hours

AGA – start in baking oven
for 30 mins then move to
simmering oven
8 – 10 hours

Rinse → Dry → toss in flour (handwritten note in margin)

PREPARATION

1. Prepare all the dried fruits and place in a bowl, add the grated orange zest, orange juice, brandy and mix well.

2. Cover and leave to soak overnight. Grease and line a 20cm-deep heart-shaped tin.

MIXING

1. Mix the glacé cherries, treacle and golden syrup into the fruit mixture on the following day and set to one side.

2. Preheat your oven if necessary.

3. Cream together the sugar and butter until light and fluffy.

4. Add the eggs one at a time with a spoonful of flour.

5. Mix in all the remaining dry ingredients and finally the soaked fruit mixture.

6. Spoon the mixture into the prepared baking tin and level the top.

BAKING

1. Bake slowly at a low temperature, in conventional ovens you may need to cover the cake during the last hour to prevent the top from burning.

2. In AGA cookers the baking starts off in the baking oven and is moved to the simmering oven. The baking time depends on the running temperature of individual AGA cookers.

3. Test the fruitcake to check that it is completely baked. Pour over a little brandy while the cake is still hot and leave in the tin to cool.

MATURING

Mature the cake at room temperature for at least four weeks, leaving the greaseproof lining paper on and wrapping in a second layer and then two layers of food wrap. Unwrap weekly to add more brandy and each time invert the cake.

DECORATING

Icing sugar for dusting
750g almond paste
4 tbsp brandy glaze

1. Lightly dust the work surface with icing sugar and knead the almond paste then roll out into a rough circle about 5cm larger than the cake (don't forget the sides need to be covered too).

2. Brush the cake with brandy glaze.

3. Gently lift the almond paste onto the top and smooth with your hands until it covers the entire cake.

4. Trim the surplus almond paste with a knife. Cover and leave to dry for 24 hours.

800g sugar paste
Edible rose buds

1. Lightly dust the work surface with icing sugar and knead then roll out the sugar paste, again 5cm larger than the cake.

2. Brush the almond paste with brandy and gently lift the sugar paste onto the cake, smoothing out with your hands until level. Trim off the surplus.

3. Cover and leave to dry for 24 hours. Decorate with edible rose buds.

DARK & STORMY GINGER FRUITCAKE

Inspiration for this cake came from our hockey tour to Bermuda in the 1980s; the combination of rum and ginger flavours works really well in this deliciously different fruitcake.

INGREDIENTS	Square tin 20cm
Sultanas	350g
Raisins	275g
Currants	225g
Lime (zest and juice)	2
Dark rum	100mls
Ginger beer	50mls
Stem ginger (finely chopped)	200g
Treacle	50g
(Stem ginger syrup	30–50g) → For icing
Demerara sugar	180g
Unsalted butter	230g
Free-range eggs	4
Plain flour	100g
Self-raising flour	180g
Mixed spice	1 tbsp
Ground ginger	1 tbsp
Ground almonds	50g
Flaked almonds	50g
Rum to pour over each week	30mls

Bake slowly at a low temperature:
Conventional oven 140c
Fan oven 120c
Gas Mark 1
2½ – 3 hours

AGA – start in baking oven for 30 mins then move to simmering oven
8 – 10 hours

PREPARATION

1. Prepare the sultanas, raisins and currants and place in a bowl. Add the grated lime zest, lime juice, rum and ginger beer and mix well.

2. Cover and leave to soak overnight. Grease and line a 20cm-diameter deep square tin.

MIXING

1. Mix in the finely chopped stem ginger and the treacle on the following day and set to one side.

2. Preheat oven if necessary.

3. Cream together the sugar and butter until light and fluffy. Add the eggs one at a time with a spoonful of flour.

4. Mix in all the remaining dry ingredients and finally the soaked fruit mixture.

5. Spoon the mixture into the prepared baking tin and level the top.

BAKING

1. Bake slowly at a low temperature; in conventional ovens you may need to cover the cake during the last hour to prevent the top from burning.

2. In AGA cookers, the baking starts off in the baking oven and is moved to the simmering oven. The baking time depends on the running temperature of individual AGA cookers.

3. Test the fruitcake to check that it is completely baked. Pour over a little rum while the cake is still hot and leave in the tin to cool.

MATURING

1. Mature the cake at room temperature for at least four weeks leaving the greaseproof paper on and wrapping in a second layer and then two layers of food wrap.

2. Unwrap weekly to add more rum and each time invert the cake.

GINGER GLACÉ ICING

INGREDIENTS

200g icing sugar (sifted)
5-6 tbsp stem ginger syrup from the jar
4-6 bulbs stem ginger (chopped)

Mix together the icing sugar and syrup until smooth and the mixture coats the back of the spoon. Pour over the cake letting it run down the sides slightly, sprinkle with finely chopped stem ginger.

WHISKY DUNDEE FRUITCAKE

Dundee fruitcakes are traditionally topped
with whole almonds and flavoured with whisky.
I would suggest you use a good malt whisky,
I believe a whisky connoisseur would easily
recognise the distinctive characteristics of
a malt whisky even in a fruitcake.

INGREDIENTS	Deep round tin 20cm diameter
Sultanas	350g
Raisins	300g
Currants	200g
Oranges *(zest and juice)*	2
Whisky	100mls
Natural-coloured cherries	100g
Treacle	50g
Golden syrup	50g
Demerara sugar	180g
Unsalted butter	230g
Free-range eggs	4
Plain flour	100g
Self-raising flour	180g
Mixed spice	1 tbsp
Ground ginger	1 tbsp
Ground almonds	50g
Flaked almonds	100g
Whisky to pour over each week	30mls

Bake slowly at a low
temperature:
Conventional oven 140c
Fan oven 120c
Gas Mark 1
2½ – 3 hours

AGA – start in baking oven for
30 mins then move to simmering
oven
8 – 10 hours

PREPARATION

1. Prepare the sultanas, raisins and currants and place in a bowl. Add the grated orange zest, orange juice, whisky and mix well.

2. Cover and leave to soak overnight.

3. Grease and line a 20cm-diameter deep round tin.

MIXING

1. Mix in the cherries, treacle and golden syrup on the following day and set to one side.

2. Preheat oven if necessary.

3. Cream together the sugar and butter until light and fluffy. Add the eggs one at a time with a spoonful of flour.

4. Mix in all the remaining dry ingredients and finally the soaked fruit mixture.

5. Spoon the mixture into the prepared baking tin and level the top.

6. If you prefer the traditional whole almond decoration, place the almonds on top of the mixture at this stage, pressing them gently into the mixture but not too far otherwise they will disappear.

BAKING

1. Bake slowly at a low temperature; in conventional ovens you may need to cover the cake during the last hour to prevent the top from burning.

2. In AGA cookers, the baking starts off in the baking oven and is moved to the simmering oven. The baking time depends on the running temperature of individual AGA cookers.

3. Test the fruitcake to check that it is completely baked. Pour over a little whisky while the cake is still hot and leave in the tin to cool.

MATURING

Mature the cake at room temperature for at least four weeks leaving the greaseproof paper on and wrapping in a second layer and then two layers of food wrap. Unwrap weekly to add more whisky and each time invert the cake.

DECORATING

100g whole blanched almonds

Traditionally whole blanched almonds are used to decorate a Dundee cake and the almonds are usually gently placed on top of the cake mixture before baking.

4 tbsp whisky glaze

500g almond paste

Thistle mould (I used a wooden shortbread mould)

Alternatively, the cake can be decorated with almond paste. Lightly dust the work surface with icing sugar and knead the almond paste, then roll out and gently press the almond paste onto the dusted mould and trim and remove. Brush the top of the cake with whisky glaze and place the moulded almond paste on top. Brown the edges with a blowtorch.

SIMNEL CAKE

Simnel cakes are steeped in history as far back as medieval times, but during the Victorian era, young girls in service would make this cake to take home on Mothering Sunday. The cake traditionally has a layer of almond paste in the middle, and is topped with almond paste and 11 balls representing the apostles (not counting Judas). Our family tradition is to make a bird's nest with shredded wheat.

INGREDIENTS	20cm round
Sultanas	350g
Raisins	300g
Currants	200g
Orange (zest and juice)	2
Brandy	100mls
Natural-coloured glacé cherries	100g
Treacle	50g
Golden syrup	50g
Demerara sugar	180g
Unsalted butter	230g
Free-range eggs	4
Plain flour	100g
Self-raising flour	180g
Mixed spice	1 tbsp
Ground almonds	50g
Flaked almonds	50g
Almond paste	900g
Brandy to pour over each week	30mls

Bake slowly at a low temperature:
Conventional oven 140c
Fan oven 120c
Gas Mark 1
2 ½ – 3 hours

AGA – start in baking oven for 30 mins then move to simmering oven
8 – 10 hours

Decorate with Almond paste, chocolate bird's nest mini eggs, crystallised flowers.

PREPARATION

1. Prepare the sultanas, raisins and currants and place in a bowl. Add the grated orange zest, orange juice and brandy and mix well.

2. Cover and leave to soak overnight. Grease and line a 20cm-diameter deep round tin.

MIXING

1. Mix in the cherries, treacle and golden syrup the following day and set to one side.

2. Preheat conventional ovens and turn on iTotal AGA cookers. Cream together the sugar and butter until light and fluffy. Add the eggs one at a time with a spoonful of flour.

3. Mix in all the remaining dry ingredients and finally the soaked fruit mixture. Spoon half of the mixture into the prepared baking tin.

4. Roll out 300g of the almond paste in a circle about 20cm wide and lay across the mixture then add the remaining mixture on top of the almond paste circle. Level the top.

BAKING

1. Bake slowly at a low temperature. In conventional ovens you may need to cover the cake during the last hour to prevent the top from burning.

2. In AGA cookers the baking starts off in the baking oven and is moved to the simmering oven. The baking time depends on the running temperature of individual AGA cookers.

3. Test the fruitcake to check that it is completely baked. Pour over a little brandy while the cake is still hot and leave in the tin to cool.

MATURING

Mature the cake at room temperature for at least four weeks, leaving the greaseproof paper on and wrapping in a second layer and then two layers of food wrap. Unwrap weekly to add more brandy and each time invert the cake.

DECORATING

1 shredded wheat
100g melted chocolate
4-5 chocolate mini eggs
Crystallised flowers from the garden

Mix the melted chocolate into the crumbled shredded wheat and make nests. Arrange the mini eggs and flowers on top and leave to set.

Brandy Glaze
2tbsp apricot jam
1-2tbsp brandy

Almond Paste
900g almond paste:
300g for the middle of cake,
300g for the top, 300g for
the 11 balls. Brown gently
with a blowtorch.

GUINNESS FRUITCAKE

Guinness is one of my favourite drinks; it is a stout made from water, barley, roasted malt extract, hops and yeast. Some of the barley is roasted giving it its characteristic colour and taste, and although not an overpowering flavour in the cake, there is definitely a malty roasted taste. One for the Guinness lovers!

INGREDIENTS	2 large loaf tins
Sultanas	350g
Raisins	275g
Currants	225g
Mixed peel	50g
Guinness	300mls
Treacle	50g
Golden syrup	50g
Soft dark brown sugar	175g
Unsalted butter	225g
Free-range eggs	4
Plain flour	100g
Self-raising flour	175g
Mixed spice	1 tbsp
Ground almonds	50g
Flaked almonds	50g
A little brandy for pouring over	

Bake slowly at a low temperature:
Conventional oven 140 c
Fan oven 120 c
Gas Mark 1
2½ – 3 hours

AGA – start in baking oven for 30 mins then move to simmering oven
8 – 10 hours

Almond paste:
750g

PREPARATION

1. Prepare the sultanas, raisins and currants and place in a bowl. Add the mixed peel and the Guinness and mix well.
2. Cover and leave to soak overnight. Grease and line 2 large loaf tins.

MIXING

1. Mix in the treacle and golden syrup on the following day and set to one side.
2. Preheat oven if necessary.
3. Cream together the sugar and butter until light and fluffy. Add the eggs one at a time with a spoonful of flour.
4. Mix in all the remaining dry ingredients and finally the soaked fruit mixture.
5. Spoon the mixture into the prepared loaf tin and level the top.

BAKING

1. Bake slowly at a low temperature. In conventional ovens you may need to cover the cake during the last hour to prevent the top from burning.
2. In AGA cookers the baking starts off in the baking oven and is moved to the simmering oven but the baking time depends on the running temperature of individual AGA cookers.
3. Test the fruitcake to check that it is completely baked. Pour over a little brandy while the cake is still hot and leave in the tin to cool.

MATURING

Mature the cake at room temperature for at least four weeks, leaving the greaseproof paper on and wrapping in a second layer and then two layers of food wrap. Decorate with 750g almond paste; make white almond paste using white castor sugar and egg whites.

SEEDED DATE & HONEY FRUITCAKE

This is the naturally sweetened/no added sugar fruitcake recipe with seeds and honey. It is a great picnic cake or perfect for a packed lunch at the half-way point of a long hike.

INGREDIENTS	2 large loaf tins
Sultanas	350g
Raisins	300g
Currants	200g
Oranges (zest and juice)	2
Brandy	100mls
Dates (chopped and made into paste with water)	180g
	4 tbsp water
Honey	100g/4 tbsp
Unsalted butter	230g
Free-range eggs	4
Plain flour	100g
Self-raising flour	180g
Mixed spice	1 tbsp
Ground almonds	50g
Flaked almonds	50g
Pumpkin seeds	50g
Sunflower seeds	50g
Brandy (to pour over cake while still hot)	30mls
Decorate: drizzle of honey and sprinkling of seeds on top	2 tbsp honey
	2 tbsp pumpkin and sunflower seeds

Bake slowly at a low temperature:
Conventional oven 140 c
Fan oven 120 c
Gas Mark 1
2½ – 3 hours

AGA – start in baking oven for 30 mins then move to simmering oven
6 – 8 hours

PREPARATION

1. Prepare the sultanas, raisins and currants and place in a bowl. Add the grated orange zest, juice and brandy and mix well.

2. Cover and leave to soak overnight.

3. Grease and line a 20cm-diameter deep round tin.

4. Cut the dates in half and place in a saucepan. Add the water and gently heat, stirring all the time until the dates become a paste. Leave to cool in a covered bowl overnight.

MIXING

1. Mix in the honey on the following day and set to one side.

2. Preheat oven if necessary.

3. Cream together the sugar and the date mixture until light and fluffy.

4. Add the eggs one at a time with a spoonful of flour.

6. Mix in all the remaining dry ingredients and finally the soaked fruit mixture.

7. Spoon the mixture into the prepared loaf tin and level the top.

BAKING

1. Bake slowly at a low temperature. In conventional ovens you may need to cover the cake during the last hour to prevent the top from burning.

2. In AGA cookers, the baking starts off in the baking oven and is moved to the simmering oven but the baking time depends on the running temperature of individual AGA cookers.

3. Test the fruitcake to check that it is completely baked.

4. Pour over a little brandy while the cake is still hot and leave in the tin to cool.

MATURING

1. Mature the cake at room temperature for at least four weeks, leaving the greaseproof paper on and wrapping in a second layer and then two layers of food wrap.

2. Unwrap weekly to add more brandy and each time invert the cake.

3. Decorate with drizzled honey and sprinkle w ith seeds.

MINI AMARETTO FRUITCAKES

These little fruitcakes have been very popular at Christmas Fairs. They make lovely little gifts tied with pretty bows in cellophane bags. I soak the fruit in brandy and add the Amaretto after baking. They are topped with a layer of almond paste and almonds but you can be as creative as you wish with decoration; you could use Amoretti biscuits instead.

INGREDIENTS	15 mini Panettone cake cases (60g or 60mm)
Sultanas	350g
Raisins	300g
Currants	200g
Orange (*zest and juice*)	2
Brandy	100mls
Treacle	50g
Golden syrup	50g
Demerara sugar	180g
Unsalted butter	230g
Free-range eggs	4
Plain flour	100g
Self-raising flour	180g
Mixed spice	1 tbsp
Ground almonds	50g
Flaked almonds	100g
Almond paste	900g
Amaretto to pour over after baking	½ tsp to each cake weekly until matured, usually after 3–4 weeks

Bake slowly at a low temperature:
Conventional oven 140c
Fan oven 120c
Gas Mark 1
1½ – 2 hours

AGA – start in baking oven for 30 mins then move to simmering oven 4 – 6 hours

PREPARATION

1. Prepare the sultanas, raisins and currants and place in a bowl. Add the grated orange zest, juice and brandy. Mix well.

2. Cover and leave to soak overnight. Grease and line 15 mini Panettone cake cases (60g or 60mm)

MIXING

1. Mix in the treacle and golden syrup the following day and set to one side.

2. Preheat conventional ovens and turn on iTotal AGA cookers.

3. Cream together the sugar and butter until light and fluffy.

4. Add the eggs one at a time with a spoonful of flour.

5. Mix in all the remaining dry ingredients and finally the soaked fruit mixture.

6. Spoon about 100g–150g of mixture into each of the cases and place them on the baking tray. Level the tops to just 1/2cm below the rim of cases.

BAKING

1. Bake slowly at a low temperature. In conventional ovens you may need to cover the cake during the last hour to prevent the top from burning.

2. In AGA cookers, the baking starts off in the baking oven and is moved to the simmering oven. The baking time depends on the running temperature of individual AGA cookers.

3. Test a cake to make sure that they are completely baked. Pour over ½ tsp Amaretto while the cakes are still hot and leave them to cool.

MATURING

1. Mature the cakes at room temperature for at least four weeks leaving them in the cases.

2. Wrap in batches of 5 with greaseproof paper and two layers of food wrap.

3. Unwrap weekly to add more Amaretto.

4. Decorate with a topping of marzipan and almonds.

ALMOND PASTE

750g Almond Paste:

Roll out the almond paste and, using a cutter the same diameter as the tops of the cakes, cut out and layer each cake and decorate with some whole almonds.

CHILLI-INFUSED VODKA & CHOCOLATE FRUITCAKE

This cake was created for my gorgeous son Matthew and his lovely fiancée Luisa. They just love this cake! Why not grow your own chillies? They are amazingly easy to grow on a window sill or in a greenhouse.

For the chilli-infused vodka:

3 large chillies
400ml bottle vodka

Remove about 20mls of vodka. Slice the washed and dried chillies into half and push them into the bottle. Put the lid on and leave for one week to infuse.

INGREDIENTS	2 large loaf tins
Sultanas	350g
Raisins	275g
Currants	125g
Chilli-infused vodka	100mls
Oranges *(zest and juice)*	2
Dark 85% coca solids chocolate	200g
Demerara sugar	175g
Unsalted butter	230g
Free-range eggs	4
Plain flour	100g
Self-raising flour	180g
Chilli flakes	1 tsp
Ground almonds	50g
Flaked almonds	50g
Extra chilli vodka *(for pouring over fruitcake after baking and during maturing)*	Approx 120mls over 4 weeks

Bake slowly at a low temperature:
Conventional oven 140c
Fan oven 120c
Gas Mark 1
2½ – 3 hours

AGA – start in baking oven for 30 mins then move to simmering oven
8 – 10 hours

PREPARATION

1. Soak the vine fruits in the chilli-infused vodka, orange zest and juice overnight.
2. Grease and line 2 large loaf tins.

MIXING

1. Mix the cake on the following day.
2. Preheat conventional ovens and turn on iTotal AGA cookers.
3. Cream together the sugar and butter until light and fluffy.
4. Add the eggs one at a time with a spoonful of flour.
5. Mix in all the remaining dry ingredients and finally the soaked fruit mixture.
6. Spoon the mixture into the prepared loaf tins and level to the tops.

BAKING

1. Bake slowly at a low temperature. In conventional ovens you may need to cover the cake during the last hour to prevent the top from burning.
2. In AGA cookers, the baking starts off in the baking oven and is moved to the simmering oven. The baking time depends on the running temperature of individual AGA cookers.
3. Test the fruitcakes to check that they are completely baked. Pour over a little chilli-infused vodka while the cakes are still hot and leave in the tins to cool.

MATURING

1. Mature the cake at room temperature for at least four weeks, leaving the greaseproof paper on and wrapping in a second layer and then two layers of food wrap.
2. Unwrap weekly to add more chilli-infused vodka .

DECORATE

Chocolate and chilli vodka drizzle

In a bowl, over a saucepan of simmering water (bain-marie), melt 200g of dark chocolate with 1 tbsp of chilli vodka and drizzle over the cake. This technique avoids the splitting and solidifying of chocolate, because it heats the chocolate gently.

WHITE FRUITCAKE

A customer at a food festival gave me the idea for this cake; she made her own fruitcakes using dried fruits but not vine fruits. My version has replaced all the vine fruits with other delicious dried fruits soaked in gin and with added white chocolate and vanilla.

INGREDIENTS	20c round tin or 20c hexagonal tin
Dried apricots	100g
Dried pineapple	200g
Dried pear	100g
Dried peach	100g
Dried apple	100g
Oranges (*zest and juice*)	2
Mixed dried peel	50g
Gin	200mls
Seeds from a vanilla pod	1
Golden caster sugar	180g
Unsalted butter	230g
Free-range eggs	4
Plain flour	100g
Self-raising flour	180g
Mixed spice	1 tbsp
Macadamia nuts	100g
Ground almonds	50g
White chocolate	100g
Gin to pour over each week	30mls
Sprinkling of grated white chocolate for decoration	25g

Bake slowly at a low temperature:
Conventional oven 140c
Fan oven 120c
Gas Mark 1
2½ – 3 hours

AGA – start in baking oven for 30 mins then move to simmering oven
8 – 10 hours

PREPARATION

1. Prepare all the dried fruits by cutting them into small pieces and placing them in a bowl. Add the grated orange zest and juice, mixed peel, gin and mix well.

2. Cover and leave to soak until all the liquid has been absorbed into the fruit.

3. Grease and line a 20cm-diameter deep round or hexagonal tin.

MIXING

1. Preheat conventional ovens.

2. Mix the seeds from one vanilla pod into the soaked fruit.

3. In a separate bowl, cream together the sugar and butter until light and fluffy. Add the eggs one at a time with a spoonful of flour.

add the eggs one at a time with a spoonful of flour.

4. Mix in all the remaining dry ingredients and finally add the soaked fruit mixture.

5. Spoon the mixture into the prepared tin and level the top.

BAKING

1. Bake slowly at a low temperature. In conventional ovens you may need to cover the cake during the last hour to prevent the top from burning.

2. In AGA cookers, the baking starts off in the baking oven and is moved to the simmering oven. The baking time depends on the running temperature of individual AGA cookers.

3. Test the fruitcake to check that it is completely baked.

4. Pour over a little gin while the cake is still hot and leave in the tin to cool.

MATURING

1. Mature the cake at room temperature for at least four weeks, leaving the greaseproof paper on and wrapping in a second layer and then two layers of food wrap. Unwrap weekly to add more gin.

2. Decorate with a sprinkling of grated white chocolate.

COINTREAU FRUITCAKE

This fruitcake is flavoured beautifully with Cointreau, Seville orange marmalade, glacé oranges and orange essence. A celebration cake that will remind you of summer holidays in Spain.

INGREDIENTS	Flower-shaped tin 20cm
Sultanas	500g
Raisins	400g
Currants	300g
Cointreau	150mls
Oranges (zest and juice)	3
Seville Orange Marmalade	150g
Orange essence	1½ tsp
Chopped glacé oranges	150g
Demerara sugar	260g
Unsalted butter	340g
Free-range eggs	6
Plain flour	150g
Self-raising flour	260g
Mixed spice	1½ tbsp
Ground almonds	75g
Flaked almonds	75g
Cointreau to pour over each week	30mls
Glacé orange slices for decoration	6

Bake slowly at a low temperature:
Conventional oven 140c
Fan oven 120c
Gas Mark 1
2½ – 3 hours

AGA – start in baking oven for 30 mins then move to simmering oven
8 – 10 hours

PREPARATION

1. Prepare the dried fruits and place in a bowl. Add the grated orange zest, juice, Cointreau and mix well.

2. Cover and leave to soak overnight.

3. Grease and line your baking tin.

MIXING

1. Mix the orange marmalade, orange essence and chopped glacé oranges into the soaked fruit

2. In a separate bowl, cream together the sugar and butter until light and fluffy.

3. Add the eggs one at a time with a spoonful of flour.

4. Mix in all the remaining dry ingredients and finally the soaked fruit mixture.

5. Spoon the mixture into the prepared tin and level the top.

BAKING

1. Bake slowly at a low temperature. In conventional ovens you may need to cover the cake during the last hour to prevent the top burning.

2. In AGA cookers the baking starts off in the baking oven and is moved to the simmering oven but the baking time depends on the running temperature of individual AGA cookers.

3. Test the fruitcake to check that it is completely baked. Pour over Cointreau while still hot and leave to cool in the tin.

MATURING

1. Mature the cake at room temperature for at least four weeks.

2. Leave the lining paper on, wrap with greaseproof paper and two layers of food wrap.

3. Unwrap weekly to add more Cointreau.

4. Decorate with slices of glacé orange.

RECIPES USING FRUITCAKE

I think we become more resourceful as we get older, and
I have developed a huge desire to reuse, recycle and reduce
and apply this to my baking too. There can be an enormous
amount of waste these days and so I am always dreaming
up new ways to use leftovers!

GINGER FRUITCAKE TRUFFLES

These make delicious after-dinner chocolates, and wrapped beautifully would also make a lovely gift.

INGREDIENTS

75g plain chocolate, melted
50mls brandy
100g traditional fruitcake, crumbled
50g ground almonds
50g finely chopped stem ginger (optional)
50g cocoa for coating
*Makes about 30 truffles

1. In a bowl, mix the crumbled fruitcake and ground almonds together, then evenly mix in the stem ginger.
2. Make a well in the centre of the mix and pour in the melted chocolate and brandy. Mix well.
3. Take a heaped teaspoon full of mixture and roll into a ball, then coat in cocoa powder.
4. Place in the fridge for 30 minutes to set.

FRUITCAKE TIRAMISU

There are so many versions of Tiramisu around and now I am adding another one. I have replaced the traditional sponge fingers with my fruitcake crumbled into the bottom of the glasses and soaked in rum and strong coffee.

1. Beat the egg yolks and sugar together for 3 minutes.
2. In a large bowl, beat the mascarpone until soft then beat in the egg and sugar mixture.
3. Whisk the egg whites in a clean bowl until soft peaks form, then fold into the mascarpone mixture. Gently mix in 1 tbsp of rum with a metal spoon.
4. Soak the crumbled fruitcake in the remaining rum and the strong coffee and spoon into the glasses. Add a layer of the mascarpone mixture and finish with chopped dark chocolate and a sprinkle of cocoa powder.

INGREDIENTS

2 egg yolks
50g golden caster sugar
250g mascarpone
2 egg whites
50mls espresso coffee or strong instant coffee
3 tbsp rum
150g traditional fruitcake, crumbled
50g dark chocolate
1tbsp cocoa
*Makes 6 in stemmed glasses

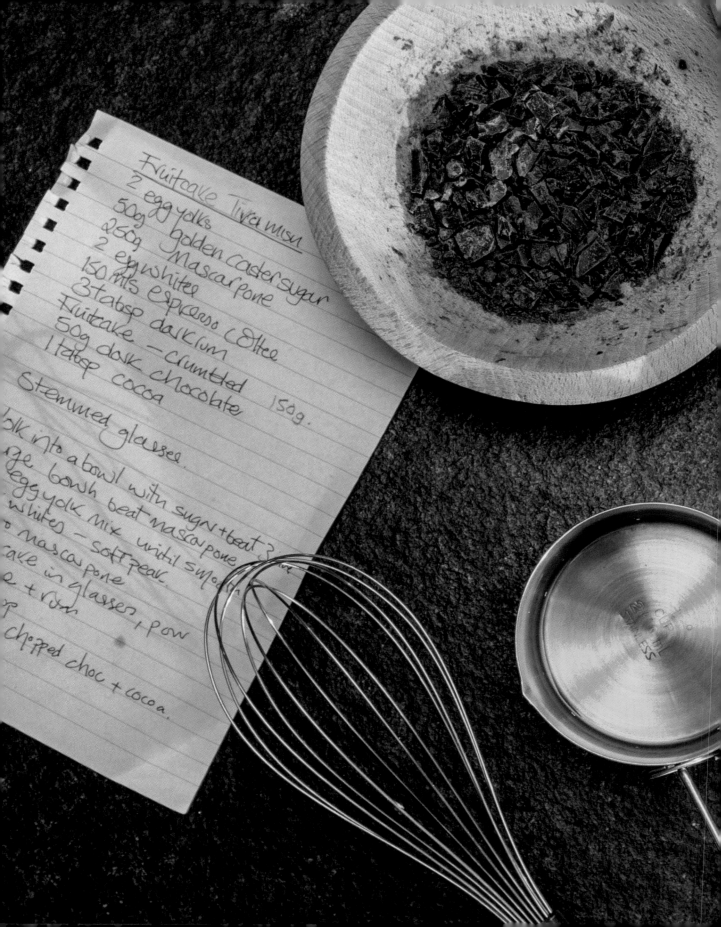

Fruitcake Tiramisu

2 egg yolks
50g golden caster sugar
250g Mascarpone
2 egg whites
150 mls espresso coffee
3 tabsp dark rum
Fruitcake — crumbled 150g.
50g dark chocolate
1 tabsp cocoa

Stemmed glasses.

yolk into a bowl with sugar + beat 3...
...ge bowl beat mascarpone
...egg yolk mix until smooth
...whites — soft peak.
...o mascarpone
...cake in glasses + pour
...e + rum
...p
chopped choc + cocoa.

HALLOWEEN FRUITCAKE POPS

Children big and small will love helping to decorate these, and if there are any left afterwards, you will have a nice supply of treats when you hear a knock on the door at Halloween.

1. Put the fruitcake crumbs into a bowl and add the melted chocolate and mix well.

2. Take a tablespoon of mixture and roll into a small ball.

3. Push a cake pop stick gently into each ball and leave to set in the fridge for 30 minutes.

4. Roll out the sugar paste thinly and cut large enough circles to cover each ball, then mould the sugar paste around the ball pressing it well onto the ball. Make a small collar from some extra sugar paste to hold it in place.

5. Leave them to dry with sticks uppermost.

6. Keep the remaining sugar paste in a plastic bag to stop it drying out. Decorate in a Halloween theme – spiders, ghosts, pumpkins and monsters – you will need plenty of little helpers at this stage, and probably plenty of tasters too.

INGREDIENTS

Crumbled fruitcake
Melted chocolate (as much as is needed to hold the fruitcake together)
Coloured sugar paste (black, green, orange and white)
Cake pop sticks

AMARETTO FRUITCAKE TRIFLE

This divine and very quick-to-make alternative to the traditional sherry trifle is surprisingly popular with the younger generation; my husband prefers it to traditional trifle, too.

1. Crumble the fruitcake into the bottom of the trifle bowl.
2. Place a layer of Amaretti biscuits on top then pour over the Amaretto and leave to soak in. The cake and biscuits should be well soaked, so add a little more Amaretto if necessary.
3. In a bowl, beat the egg yolks and sugar together until thick and pale; this will take around 3 minutes.
4. Gently heat the milk and vanilla seeds to simmering point in a saucepan.
5. Gradually pour the simmered milk into the egg mixture but keep stirring. Pour back into the saucepan and heat gently until it thickens, but don't let it boil or the egg will coagulate.
6. Allow to cool before pouring over the cake and biscuit mixture and allow the custard to set in the fridge for 30 minutes.
7. Whisk the double cream until soft peaks form, then gently whisk in the amaretto and pour over the set custard. Sprinkle with the toasted flaked almonds.

INGREDIENTS

250g crumbled traditional fruitcake
100mls Amaretto
100g Amaretti biscuits

FOR CUSTARD
(works well with 500mls of ready-made custard too)

450mls milk
3 eggs yolks
100g golden caster sugar
Seeds from 1 vanilla pod

FOR TOPPING

300mls double cream
2 tbsp Amaretto
50g toasted flaked almonds

KIRSCH FRUITCAKE ICE CREAM

Every freezer should have a home-made ice cream stored away in it. I recommend this custard-based fruitcake and Kirsch ice cream. If you are in a rush, ready-made custard works too, but if you make your own custard remember not to let it boil, otherwise you will end up with scrambled egg!

1. In a bowl, beat the egg yolks and sugar together until thick and pale; this will take around 3 minutes.

2. Gently heat the cream to simmering point in a saucepan.

3. Gradually pour the simmered cream into the egg mixture but keep stirring. Pour back into the saucepan and heat gently until it thickens, but don't let it boil or the egg will coagulate.

4. Pour into a bowl and allow to cool.

5. When cool, add the Kirsch-soaked fruitcake and chopped glacé cherries to the mixture.

6. Beat the double cream and fold into the mixture.

7. Pour into a freezer container and freeze, mixing the mixture every hour for 3 hours.

*Custard-based ice creams need 3 to 4 hours total freezing time. Remember to remove from the freezer 30 minutes before serving.

INGREDIENTS

450mls single cream

3 egg yolks

100g caster sugar

150ml double cream

100g fruitcake

2 tbsp Kirsch

50g chopped natural glacé cherries

FRUITCAKE PALATHAI

Palathai means 'cakes made with squashed figs'. I have tasted many versions of Palathai as this old Roman recipe is still made in Turkey and Eastern Europe today. My version uses fruitcake which makes it less sticky.

INGREDIENTS

400g dried soft figs
200g crumbled fruitcake
2 tsp coriander seeds (ground)
50g ground pistachio nuts

1. Use a soft variety of dried figs as the harder figs contain crunchy pips. Remove the stalks from the figs and push through a fine mincer, pulse in a blender, or mash in a pestle and mortar.
2. Mix the crumbled fruitcake and figs and shape with your hands into an oval cake.
3. Mix the ground pistachio nuts and coriander and dust the outside of the cake.
4. Serve in small wedges.

FRUITCAKE M'HANNACHA

I have added a fruitcake centre to this traditional Moroccan dessert, which is also known as 'snake cake' because of its coiled shape. It usually contains citrus and rose flavours and is decorated with chopped nuts and rose petals.

1. In a bowl, mix the crumbled fruitcake, orange zest, cloves and rose water.

2. Roll the almond paste into 6 x 15cm long pieces (about the same length as the filo pastry) and flatten to about 3cm wide.

3. Place a small amount of the fruitcake mixture along the centre of each almond paste piece and enclose the fruitcake gently using your fingers to squash the paste together.

4. Brush 6 filo sheets with melted butter on a lightly flour-dusted surface, joining them end to end, overlapping by 1cm. Place the 6 remaining sheets on top to form a second layer and brush again with melted butter.

5. Place the almond paste rolls end to end at the edge of the filo sheets and gently roll the whole cake into a coil like a snake. Brush with melted butter.

6. Place on a baking sheet and bake for 15mins until golden brown.

7. Leave to cool before decorating with a dusting of icing sugar and sprinkling of pistachio nuts and fresh rose petals. Cut to serve, or break and share as they do in Morocco.

INGREDIENTS

12 sheets of filo pastry sheets

1kg almond paste

2 tsp rose water

500g fruitcake, crumbled

Zest of 1 orange

A pinch of ground cloves

150g unsalted butter (melted)

Decorate with:

Icing sugar to dust

Pistachios nuts

Fresh rose petals from the garden

Preheat:

Conventional oven 180c

Fan oven 160c

Gas Mark 4

AGA – roasting oven floor

BAKED APPLES WITH FRUITCAKE CENTRES

The secret with this recipe is making sure the apples are cooled before applying the pastry, otherwise it will just fall off the apple. This is great for using up those surplus autumn apples.

1. Rub the butter into the flour with your fingertips until it resembles fine breadcrumbs.

2. Add water and mix until the dough begins to hold together; add a little more water if needs be until you have a soft dough. Wrap in cling film and cool in the fridge.

3. Wash then remove the cores of the apples. Cut about 1cm off the bottom of each core to use as a stopper. Pierce the apple skin a few times with a sharp knife.

4. Wrap each apple in a piece of foil and place in an ovenproof dish. Bake in the oven until just soft, about 30 minutes depending on the size of the apples. Allow to cool completely.

5. Crumble the fruitcake and mix with the cinnamon and fill the centre of each apple.

6. Save a little pastry to cut out 4 leaf shapes. Roll out the rest of the pastry and cut into strips 25mm wide.

7. Beginning at the top of each apple, press the pastry firmly round in a spiral, overlapping the edges until the whole apple is covered. Tuck the end of the strip under the apple. Place a leaf-shaped piece on the top.

8. Put the apples into an ovenproof dish. Brush with melted butter and sprinkle with golden caster sugar.

9. Bake for 15–20 minutes. Serve hot with single cream or plain yoghurt.

FOR THE PASTRY

100g unsalted butter (cut into small pieces straight from the fridge)
200g plain flour
3tbsp cold water
4 large baking apples equally sized
200g fruitcake
1 teaspoon cinnamon
50g unsalted butter, melted

Preheat:
Conventional oven 160c
Fan oven 140c
Gas Mark 3

AGA – Roasting Oven lowest shelf

BRITISH CLASSIC FRUITCAKES

I have happy memories of baking as a child and many of those memories are of baking the British classics. These recipes are the bedrock of our learning; they tell a story, are innovative in their own time, and every one is steeped in tradition.

BARA BRITH

Traditional Welsh fruit loaf made by soaking the vine fruits in strong black tea; the name translates to 'speckled bread'.

1. Soak the dried fruit in tea overnight.

2. Mix the flour, sugar and spice together in a large bowl and make a well in the middle. Add the egg, grated orange rind and juice, honey and the soaked fruit mix. Mix well.

3. Pour into a lined square tin and bake for 1¾ to 2 hours. Depending on individual ovens you may have to cover the top with some foil for the last hour to prevent burning.

INGREDIENTS

450g mixed dried fruit

300mls strong black tea

450g self-raising flour (sifted)

175g muscovado sugar

2 tsp mixed spice

1 egg

25g honey

1 orange (grated rind and juice)

Deep 15cm square baking tin or large loaf tin lined with greaseproof paper

Preheat: Conventional oven 160c
Fan oven 140c Gas Mark 3

AGA – bottom shelf of baking oven

EARL GREY ENGLISH TEA BREAD

This is a typical English Tea Bread. After a recent visit to Howick Hall in Northumberland, the family seat of the Grey Family, I learnt that Earl Grey tea was specially blended by a Chinese Mandarin for Lord Grey using bergamot to offset the lime in the local water. Fresh bergamot, if you can get hold of it, would be a great addition to this recipe.

INGREDIENTS

175g sultanas

175g raisins

225g muscovado sugar

300mls strong hot Earl Grey tea

275g Self-raising flour (sifted)

1 egg (beaten)

Prepare a greased and lined 900g loaf tin

Preheat: Conventional oven 160c

Fan over 140c / Gas Mark 3

AGA – baking oven

1. Mix all the ingredients together in a large bowl and pour into baking tin.

2. Bake for 1 to 1 ½ hours. Cool on wire rack.

BLACK BUN

Traditionally a Scottish fruitcake covered in shortcrust pastry, this was originally the Scottish version of Twelfth Night Cake but has subsequently become a Hogmanay cake, delivered along with other gifts by the 'first footer' – the first person to enter the household on New Years' Day.

1. Rub the butter into the flour with your fingertips until it resembles fine breadcrumbs.

2. Add the water and mix until the dough begins to hold together; if it is too dry add a little more water and mix until you have a soft dough.

3. Wrap in cling film and cool in the fridge while you make the filling.

4. Set aside a beaten egg and some golden caster sugar for finishing. Place all the other ingredients into a large mixing bowl and mix them together well.

5. On a lightly floured board, roll out two-thirds of the pastry.

6. Gently line the tin with the pastry, being careful not to rip it. Spoon the filling onto the pastry in the tin and press down firmly. Lightly brush the pastry edges with water.

7. Roll out the remaining third of pastry, place on top and press around the edge with a fork. Cut off excess pastry, decorate with a pastry thistle, brush with the beaten egg and sprinkle with golden caster sugar.

8. Bake for 2 hours. You may have to cover with foil for the last ½ hour to prevent burning. Leave to cool on a wire rack. Store for up to 1 month in an airtight container.

FOR THE PASTRY

100g unsalted butter (cut into small pieces straight from the fridge) 200g plain flour
3 tbsp cold water

FOR THE FILLING

200g plain flour
100g soft dark sugar
400g currants
200g raisins
100g mixed dried peel
50g ground almonds
50g flaked almonds
3 eggs (1 for brushing over pastry)
3 tbsp milk
60mls whisky
1 tsp ground ginger
1 tsp ground cinnamon
½ tsp cayenne pepper
½ tsp of bicarbonate of soda
Large loaf tin greased with butter
1 tsp golden caster sugar for sprinkling

Preheat:
Conventional oven 180c
Fan oven 160c
Gas Mark 4

AGA – middle shelf of baking oven

'BROWNIE BADGE' ROCK CAKES

I baked these very traditional English cakes at the age of 7 for my first Brownie badge, and every time I bake them I am transported back in time! They are best eaten on the day they are baked but they freeze very well.

1. Rub the butter into the flour with your fingertips until it resembles fine breadcrumbs.

2. Stir in the sugar, nutmeg and fruit.

3. Beat the egg with the milk in a small bowl.

4. Make a well in the middle of the mix and add the beaten egg and milk and mix the dough until it roughly holds together, add more milk if too dry.

5. Shape the dough into 12 mounds on a lined baking tray.

6. Sprinkle with the extra sugar and bake for 15 minutes until pale golden brown at the edges.

INGREDIENTS

100g butter

200g Self-raising flour

100g demerara sugar (and extra for sprinkling)

100g mixed dried fruits

50g mixed dried peel

1 egg

1 tbsp milk

1 tsp nutmeg

Baking tray lined with greaseproof paper

Preheat:

Conventional oven 200c

Fan oven 180c / Gas Mark 6

AGA – bottom shelf roasting oven

WELSHCAKES

These cakes are so quick and easy to make, they remind me of NCT coffee mornings when my children were young and we lived in Wales. We often had a house full of mums, babies and toddlers. I served them warm spread with butter, or cold sprinkled with caster sugar.

INGREDIENTS

100g unsalted butter *(cut into small pieces)*

200g self-raising flour *(sifted)*

75g golden caster sugar

100g vozzitia currants *(any currants will do but vozzitia are the best)*

1 tsp mixed spice

1 egg

1 tbsp milk

1. Rub the butter into the flour with your fingertips until it resembles fine breadcrumbs.
2. Mix in the sugar, currants and spices.
3. Beat the egg with the milk in a small bowl.
4. Make a well in the middle of the flour mixture and pour in the egg and milk, then mix to form a firm dough (add more milk if necessary).
5. Roll the dough out onto a lightly-floured surface to 5mm thick and cut into rounds using a cutter.
6. Cook on a lightly oiled griddle on a low heat or straight onto the lightly oiled AGA simmering plate for 3 minutes each side, until golden brown.

IRISH BOILED FRUITCAKE

With quite a few Irish relatives I had to include an Irish fruitcake! This is a lovely light fruitcake, I am often asked about boiled fruitcakes at food festivals; boiled fruitcakes tend to be moist and they keep for several days if stored in an airtight container.

1. In a saucepan, gently heat the butter and sugar, stirring to dissolve the sugar.
2. Add the stout and the dried fruit and simmer for 10 minutes. Leave to cool.
3. When cool enough, mix in the eggs and then fold in the flour, spices and cocoa powder and mix well.
4. Pour into the prepared cake tin and bake for 2 ½ to 3 hours. You may have to cover with foil towards the end of baking to prevent burning.
5. When a skewer comes out clean, place on a wire rack and pour over the Irish whisky then leave to cool. Serve with a dusting of icing sugar or a sugar paste shamrock using heart-shaped cutters.

INGREDIENTS

115g unsalted butter
115g demerara sugar
150mls stout
75g sultanas
75g raisins
75g currants
2 eggs (beaten)
225g self-raising flour
1 teaspoon mixed spice
1 teaspoon cocoa powder
Dusting of icing sugar
1 tbsp Irish whisky (to pour over while cake is still hot)
Prepared greased and lined 15cm round deep tin

Preheat:
Conventional oven 160c
Fan oven 140c
Gas Mark 3

AGA – lowest shelf baking oven

HOT CROSS BUNS

These sweet and spiced buns are marked with a cross on the top, and are traditionally eaten hot or toasted during Lent – from Shrove Tuesday until Good Friday.

1. Soak the dried fruit in the hot black tea.

2. Mix the flour, sugar, spices and yeast in a large bowl. Make a well and pour in the tepid milk and beaten eggs. Mix well to form a soft dough.

3. Knead for 10 minutes until the dough is elastic. Leave to rise for an hour. Add the strained dried fruit.

4. Divide into 16 and shape into rolls. Place on a baking sheet. Cover with a damp cloth and leave to rise until doubled in size.

5. For the cross, mix the flour and water until smooth, then pour into a plastic freezer bag. Cut a small hole across the corner and pipe a cross onto each bun.

6. Bake in the oven for 15 minutes, turning halfway through baking.

7. Tap the bottom of the buns to check they are baked and cool on a wire rack.

INGREDIENTS

50g raisins

50g sultanas

50g currants

50g mixed peel

100mls strong hot black tea

400g strong plain flour

1 tablespoon easy bake dried yeast

200mls tepid milk

50g golden caster sugar

½ teaspoon salt

50g unsalted butter *(cut into small pieces)*

3 eggs *(beaten)* 2 for the dough and 1 for glazing

1 tablespoons mixed spice

FOR THE CROSS

3 tablespoons of flour

2 tablespoons water

Plastic freezer bag

Preheat: Conventional oven 200c Fan oven 180c / Gas Mark 6

AGA – roasting oven with grid shelf on bottom

ECCLES CAKES

These delicious and world famous cakes made with currants and flaky pastry, are named after the village of Eccles near Manchester.

1. Cut the butter into 4 pieces and rub one of the pieces into the flour and salt. Add the lemon juice and water (you may not need it all) to make a soft but not sticky pastry. Use a palette knife for mixing.

2. Turn the pastry out onto a lightly-floured board and knead very lightly, creating a smooth pastry. Wrap in a plastic bag and leave to relax in the fridge for 20 minutes.

3. Gently press and roll the cooled pastry on a lightly-floured board. You want a rectangle about 5mm thick.

4. Mark the rectangle into thirds, take another piece of butter and arrange small dots over ⅔ of the pastry. Fold the ends over so the plain ⅓ is in the middle.

5. Quarter turn the pastry and seal the open edges with a rolling pin. Repeat this process twice more, always with the folded sides to the left, using up the other two pieces of butter and once more without butter, so rolling and folding 4 times in all.

6. Wrap in a plastic bag again and rest in the fridge while you assemble the filling.

7. Set aside a beaten egg and some golden caster sugar for finishing. Place all the other ingredients into a large mixing bowl and mix them together well.

8. Roll the pastry into a rectangle 30cm x 60cm and cut into 8 squares. Divide the filling between the squares and brush the edges with beaten egg then fold in the corners and squeeze together gently until brushed edges are sealed. Turn over and shape into circles, flatten a little with a rolling pin and make 3 cuts across the top. Brush with beaten egg and sprinkle with golden caster sugar.

INGREDIENTS

For the flaky pastry:
150g butter
200g plain flour (sifted)
1/4 teaspoon salt
2 tsp lemon juice
125ml water

FOR THE FILLING

50g butter
150g currants
50g mixed peel
50g golden caster sugar
1 tsp mixed spice
Large baking tray
1 egg (beaten for brushing)
Caster sugar for sprinkling

Preheat:
Conventional oven 220c
Fan oven 210c
Gas Mark 7

AGA – roasting oven
*Makes approx 8 cakes

9. Place on a baking tray. Bake for 10 – 15 minutes until golden. Leave to cool on the baking tray for 5 minutes before transferring to a wire rack to cool completely.

TWELFTH NIGHT CAKE

This celebration cake is associated with a long history. Many years ago it was customary to celebrate Twelfth Night on 5th January (the last day of Christmas) with a big party. In Victorian times the cake was made using the Pound Cake recipe – a pound of butter, pound of sugar and pound of flour. A dried bean would be put into the right half of the cake and a dried pea would be put into the left, and whoever got the bean would be King for the night and whoever got the pea would be Queen! Victorian fruitcakes would often contain exotic spices from the East, and these where considered to be gifts from the Wise Men. In addition to vine fruits, Victorian fruitcakes also contained large quantities of glacé fruits.

1. Soak the vine fruits in brandy overnight.
2. Prepare a greased and lined 25cm round deep loose-bottomed tin.
3. Cream the butter and sugar until light and fluffy. Mix in the eggs one at a time with a spoonful of flour, then add the rest of the flour, spices and almonds and mix well. Add the vine fruits and glacé fruits and mix well.
4. Pour mix into prepared tin and bake for 2 ½ to 3 hours, covering with foil towards to end of baking if necessary.
5. Test with a skewer in middle and if it comes out clean remove from oven and cool in the tin on a cooling rack.
6. Pour over 2 tablespoons of brandy while hot if you wish, straight from oven and cool in the tin on a wire rack.

INGREDIENTS

450g mixed dried vine fruits
100ml brandy
450g unsalted butter
450g dark muscovado sugar
8 eggs
450g Self-Raising flour (sifted)
2 tablespoons mixed spice
100g ground almonds
100g flaked almond
450g glacé/crystallised fruits (chopped)

Preheat:
Conventional oven 160c
Fan oven 140c
Gas Mark 3
2 ½ to 3 hours.

AGA –lowest shelf baking oven for 5 – 6 hours

DECORATING

Use an almond paste base layer and a rough royal icing covering, topped with whole glacé fruits and edible gold leaf.

FRESH FRUITCAKES

I look forward to our four British seasons with equal measure. Winter, spring, summer or autumn, there is always a fruitcake to make, a party to plan or a family gathering to enjoy. I am always inspired to use produce from my garden in my fruitcakes, but using fresh fruits will reduce the keeping quality so these cakes are best stored in the freezer.

CARROT CAKE

I like to use my own home-grown carrots in this recipe because they are simply tastier than shop-bought carrots. This is a lovely moist cake and will keep for a week and it also freezes well. Carrots are surprisingly easy to grow, for a good crop all you need is a well-dug plot with fine stone-free soil. Sow in the autumn for a spring crop, or in early spring for summer crop. Thin them out until about 10cm apart.

1. Grease and line a 15cm-deep round tin. Beat together the sugar, sunflower oil and eggs and stir in the sifted flour, spices and bicarbonate of soda. Then add the carrots, sultanas and pecans.

2. Spoon the mixture into the cake tin and bake for 1 -1 ½ hours, or 1 hour in the AGA baking oven.

FOR THE SYRUP:
2 oranges (rind and juice)
100g soft brown sugar

To make the syrup, stir the zest and juice of the oranges with the sugar over a gentle heat until dissolved. As soon as the cake comes out of the oven, slowly pour over the syrup while the cake is still hot; you will need to place a tray under the tin to catch any syrup that may run straight through. If necessary freeze at this stage.

INGREDIENTS
150g soft brown sugar
150mls sunflower oil
2 eggs
175g plain flour
2 tsp mixed spice
2 tsp bicarbonate of soda
200g carrots
100g sultanas
50g pecan nuts

Preheat:
Conventional oven 160c
Fan oven 140c
Gas Mark 3

AGA – baking oven bottom shelf

Optional cream cheese frosting

INGREDIENTS

250g tub of mascarpone
50g caster sugar
1 carrot (finely grated)
1 orange (grated zest)

1. Beat the mascarpone and sugar together until light and fluffy, then spread on top of the cake.
2. Finely grate some carrot and orange rind directly over the cream cheese frosting.

APPLE BAKED CHEESECAKE

I love baked cheesecakes and this is a lovely apple and dried fruit version. It looks like a Normandy-style cheesecake with the glazed apples on top, and tastes like bread and butter pudding. Best eaten warm on the day it's baked.

For the base of cake
INGREDIENTS

75g butter
50g golden caster sugar
100g crushed digestive biscuits
50g finely chopped almonds

1. Grease a loose bottom 20cm-round cake tin. Melt the butter and sugar in a saucepan, then stir in the biscuits and almonds.
2. Pour into the cake tin, press down and level and cool in the fridge.

For the soaked fruit mixture
INGREDIENTS

25g chopped natural glacé cherries
75g mixed dried fruits
1 orange (rind and juice)
2tbsp brandy

Soak the cherries and dried fruits in the orange juice, juice, grated rind and brandy

For the cheesecake
INGREDIENTS

225g curd cheese
3 egg yolks
100g golden caster sugar
1 tsp mixed spice
30g plain flour
150mls double cream
3 egg whites
1 desert apple, sliced
15cm round deep loose bottom tin
Preheat conventional oven 160c
fan oven 140c
Gas Mark 3
AGA – baking oven

1. Beat and soften the cheese in a large bowl, then beat in the egg yolks, sugar, spice, flour, soaked fruits and cream.
2. In a clean bowl whisk the egg whites until stiff, then fold into the cheese mixture. Spoon into cake tin on top of biscuit base, and arrange sliced apple on top.
3. Bake the cheesecake until firm but spongy, for 1½ to 1¾ hours.

For the glazed topping
INGREDIENTS

2 tbsp apricot jam
2 tbsp brandy
When cool, glaze with apricot jam and brandy.

HOMEMADE APPLE MINCEMEAT CAKE

This delicious quick and easy cake was the first cake I baked in my first AGA cooker, the recipe was given to me at a local AGA demonstration. I have altered it a bit over the years, I add more mincemeat and use the creaming method rather than the all-in-one method. I recently discovered it was Mary Berry who invented the original mincemeat cake.

INGREDIENTS FOR THE MINCEMEAT

250g stewed cooking apples

2 tbsp water

knob of butter

200g shredded beef suet, vegetable suet or grated cold butter

200g raisins

200g currants

200g sultanas

150g mixed peel

100g glacé cherries

50g flaked almonds

1 orange (grated rind and juice)

1 tsp mixed spice

100g dark brown sugar

100mls brandy

*Makes 3 x 400g jars

FOR THE CAKE:

100g unsalted butter

100g golden caster sugar

2 eggs

200g self-raising flour

2 tbsp milk

6 tbsp mincemeat

Flaked almonds for decoration

2 small loaf tins lined with greaseproof paper

AGA baking oven, Conventional 160c, Fan 140c, Gas Mark 3.

Mincemeat is a traditional preserve. It was originally made with minced meat, often tongue, mixed with dried fruits and a lot of spice. The meat has been replaced with suet these days, and again many people prefer to use vegetable suet or grated cold butter. Packed down firmly in sterilized jars with screw-top lids will prevent it from drying out. As with rich fruitcakes, the flavour develops after a week or two so remember to make it ahead of time.

MINCEMEAT

1. Mix all the ingredients together thoroughly, and pack into sterilized cold jars. Press down well, and cover with screw top lid.

2. Suet aids the keeping property of the mincemeat by coating the fruits and sealing them preventing fermentation. This will keep for 6 months if store in cool dry place.

CAKE

3. Cream the butter and sugar together until light and fluffy then add the eggs one at a time with a spoonful of flour, then add the milk and fold in the flour.

4. Gently mix in the mincemeat. Divide the mixture between 2 small loaf tins. Level the top and sprinkle with the flaked almonds.

5. Bake for 45-50 minutes.

HARVEST CAKE

It is hard to use up all the fruits of the harvest, but use our freezer to capacity to stash away our fresh produce. This cake was inspired simply by the need to use up apples, pears and our black and redcurrants. Because we freeze a lot of our produce, I can make this cake any time of year!

1. Prepare a 23cm loose bottom tin, lined with greaseproof paper.

2. In a large bowl, gently stir together the fruits, nuts and seeds with the flour, baking powder and sugar. Beat the eggs with the oil and add to the dry ingredients. Stir until well mixed.

3. Turn half the mixture into the prepared tin and level. Crumble the cheese over the mixture.

4. Add the remaining mixture.

5. Bake for 50 – 60 minutes until just firm. Cool in the tin for 5 minutes then remove from tin and transfer to a wire rack to cool completely.

INGREDIENTS

125g apple (*peeled, cored and chopped*)

125g pear (*peeled cored and chopped*)

125g blackcurrants

125 redcurrants

100g sultanas

100g raisins

75g walnuts

50 sunflower seeds

175g self-raising flour (*sifted*)

1teaspoon baking powder

75g golden caster sugar

2 eggs

90mls sunflower oil

150g Wensleydale cheese

Icing sugar for dusting

Preheat:
Conventional oven 160c
Fan oven 140c
Gas Mark 3

AGA – baking oven

SHROPSHIRE DAMSON CAKE

The Shropshire Damson is a very old variety of small plum-like fruits with a distinctive rich and astringent taste. Charles Darwin famously compared the stones of plums in his book, *Variation of Animals and Plants under Domestication*. We are lucky to have Shropshire damson trees in our hedges, and the harvest is usually plentiful from August to September. I am often busy making jam, chutney and damson gin in the summer. It makes a change to bake a cake with the damsons. Serve with a dollop of crème fraîche and a drizzle of damson sauce.

1. Soak the damsons and sultanas in the damson gin overnight.

2. Cream the sugar and butter together until light and fluffy. Mix in the seeds from the vanilla pod.

3. Add the eggs a little at time, with a little flour to prevent curdling.

4. Mix in the yoghurt.

5. Fold in the flour.

6. Spoon 1/3 of the mixture into the tin.

7. Into the remaining mixture, fold in the soaked damsons and sultanas.

8. Fill the tin with remaining mixture and level top.

9. Bake for 1 hour to 1 1/2 hours.

INGREDIENTS

100g damsons (*with stones removed*)
100g sultanas
45mls damson gin
250g muscovado sugar
250g unsalted butter
1 vanilla pod (*seeds*)
5 eggs (*lightly beaten*)
100g Greek yoghurt
350g self-raising flour (*sifted*)

20cm loose bottom tin lined with greaseproof paper

Preheat:
Conventional oven 160c
Fan oven 140c
Gas Mark 3
AGA – baking oven

1 – 1 ½ hours (until a skewer dipped in the middle comes out clean)

DAMSON GIN

INGREDIENTS

500g damsons *(don't use bruised or overripe ones)*
Demijohn or large jar
250g granulated sugar *(for a more syrupy Gin use 500g)*
1 litre gin

1. Prick the damson all over with a fork and put into a sterilized jar.
2. Add the sugar and gin and give it a swirl every day to help the sugar dissolve.
3. After 3 months, strain to remove the fruit and pour into sterilised bottles.

DAMSON SAUCE

INGREDIENTS

100g damsons
50g sugar
2 tbsp water
1 tbsp damson gin

1. Simmer the damsons, sugar and water over a low heat until soft.
2. Strain to remove stones and add the damson gin.

HEDGEROW CAKE

I love our hedgerows – they burst into life during the spring and play a very important role for our wildlife. I decided to make this cake as a celebration of nature's larder and hedgerow foraging. Using berries like blackberries, raspberries, and combining these with cobnuts and the scent of rose will always remind me of home.

1. Soak the sultanas in the tea overnight, and drain well.
2. Cream the butter and sugar until light and fluffy. Add the eggs one at time with a spoonful of flour then add the remaining sifted flour and mix in the rose water.
3. In a separate bowl mix the topping ingredients.
4. Pour half the cake mixture into the tin. Make a layer of raspberries and blackberries and well-drained sultanas. Gently cover the fruit layer with the remaining half of cake mixture.
5. Scatter the topping mixture on top of the cake and bake. Cover with foil if browning too quickly on top.

INGREDIENTS

75g sultanas
100mls jasmine or rose tea
150g unsalted butter
150g golden caster sugar
3 eggs
150g self-raising flour (sifted)
1 tsp rose water
75g blackberries
75g raspberries

TOPPING:

75g honey
30g unsalted butter (melted)
50g rolled oats
50g chopped hazelnuts or cobnuts

Prepared a greased and lined 15cm deep tin

Preheat:
Conventional oven 160c
Fan oven 140c
Gas Mark 3
AGA baking oven

1 – 1 1/2 hours (until a skewer dipped in the middle comes out clean)

LAVENDER & BANANA CAKE

Lavender is the perfect cottage garden plant. It belongs to the mint family, Lamiaceae, and it grows well in our sunny garden. There are many culinary uses for it –from flavouring cakes and sugar, to decoration and garnish, and delicious honey made when bees collect nectar from lavender.

1. Rub the butter into the flour with your fingertips until it resembles fine breadcrumbs.

2. Peel and mash the bananas, and stir into the flour with the sugar, lemon zest and eggs.

3. Beat well and turn into prepared tin. Level the surface and bake.

4. You may need to cover with foil towards the end of baking to prevent it from browning too much.

5. Cool in the tin for 5 minutes then turn out onto a wire rack to cool completely. Sprinkle with lavender sugar to serve.

FOR THE CAKE

100g butter
225g self-raising flour
225g bananas
100g lavender sugar
1 lemon (*zest*)
2 eggs

FOR LAVENDER SUGAR

500g sugar
2-3 tablespoons of lavender flowers
Mix together and store in a clip sealed jar for a week before using.

Large 900g loaf tin lined with greaseproof paper

Preheat:
Conventional oven 160c
Fan oven 140c
Gas Mark 3
AGA baking oven

1 – 1 1/2 hours (until a skewer dipped in the middle comes out clean)

COURGETTE & CARDAMOM CAKE

Courgettes or zucchini always grow so well in my garden, it is very tempting to grow too many and then run out of space! The seeds are planted sideways into pots of compost in the spring and grow on a window ledge or in the greenhouse until the young plants are ready to be transplanted to the vegetable plot. The flowers are edible too. Smaller courgettes are tastier and with lime and cardamom they make a great cake.

1. Soak the sultanas overnight in the lime zest and juice.

2. Open the cardamom pods and remove the seeds and grind in a pestle and mortar.

3. To make the cake, mix the oil, sugar and eggs together in a bowl.

4. In a separate bowl mix together the flour, ground cardamom seeds, coconut, almonds and bicarbonate of soda. Add the grated courgette and egg mixture. Mix well.

5. Pour into the prepared tin and bake. You may want to cover the cake with foil during the last 30 minutes of baking to prevent burning.

7. Make the syrup by combining the sugar and lime juice over a gentle heat and pour over the cake while it's still hot. Cool on a wire rack.

INGREDIENTS

100g sultanas
2 limes (rind and juice)
2 tsp cardamom pods
150mls sunflower oil
150g golden caster sugar
2 eggs
175g plain flour, sifted
50g desiccated coconut
50g flaked almonds
1 tsp bicarbonate of soda
175g coarsely-grated courgette
(about 1 medium-sized)

FOR THE SYRUP

75g caster sugar
Juice of 2 limes

Grease and line a 15cm deep round tin

Preheat:
Conventional oven 160c
Fan oven 140c
Gas Mark 3
AGA – baking oven lowest shelf

1 – 1 1/2 hours (until a skewer dipped in the middle comes out clean)

BEETROOT & CHOCOLATE CAKE

Beetroot is a little harder to grow but is well worth the try. It has healthy quantities of iron and minerals and has been classified as a super food. A boltardy variety is the most successful. The young leaves are great to eat too. Sow in April straight into growing position and thin out until 10cm apart. Contemporary bakers are making bright red cakes using beetroot these days; beetroot fruitcakes are a lovely rich dark colour and with the dark chocolate it is a great combination.

1. Soak the sultanas overnight in the orange zest and juice.

2. To make the cake, mix the oil, sugar and eggs together in a bowl.

3. In a separate bowl, mix together the flour, chocolate, spices and bicarbonate of soda. Add the grated beetroot and the egg mixture. Mix well.

4. Pour into the prepared tin and bake. You may want to cover the cake with foil during the last 30 minutes of baking to prevent burning.

5. Make the syrup by combining the sugar and orange juice over a gentle heat and pour over the cake while it's still hot. Cool on a wire rack.

INGREDIENTS

100g sultanas

1 orange (rind and juice)

150mls sunflower oil

150g soft brown sugar

2 eggs

175g plain flour

100g dark chocolate (*75% cocoa solids*)

2 tsp cinnamon

1 tsp nutmeg

2 tsp bicarbonate of soda

175g beetroot (*coarsely grated*)

FOR THE SYRUP:

75g caster sugar

Juice of 1 orange

Grease and line a 15cm deep round tin

Preheat:
Conventional oven 160c
Fan oven 140c
Gas Mark 3
AGA baking oven bottom shelf

1 – 1 1/2 hours (a skewer dipped in the middle should be clean apart from melted chocolate)

INDEX